Recommer ...uns

"There are heaps of books on leadership but few as entertaining as Peter Hawkins'. I get tired of the rather dry and academic tones. You can always learn a huge amount about leadership from stories. After all, we are often judged on our own leadership by the stories that are told about us. Read, mark and inwardly digest ... and have a laugh as you read this."

Stephen Bubb, Chief Executive of ACEVO (Association of Chief Executives of Voluntary Organizations).

"In the current complex political climate leadership is everything. This book reminds us that leadership is the most human of challenges, and through the stories and vignettes it connects us with the humility, empathy and intelligence which we all need to lead ourselves as well as others."

Lord Victor Adebowale, CBE, Chief Executive of *Turning Point*.

"In running a number of businesses and sitting on Boards of a number of international companies, I constantly see the mistakes leaders make in attending to things. Life is fundamentally about relationships not things. The problems lie in the interfaces, between organisations, between teams and between people. So do the opportunities. This book helps us to turn our attention from seeing things to seeing relationships. I recommend it as a great source of stories and insights for not only executives but also board members."

Dr. Paul Cluver, Chairman of Capespan: Wines of South Africa, and Vinfuco. Board member of Fyffes. Board member at the universities of Cape Town and Stellenbosch. Previously a leading brain surgeon.

"Peter Hawkins has achieved a brilliant synthesis of old folk wisdom and the modern day management environment. Nasrudin, the archetypal wise fool, dons the management consultant's hat and reminds the corporate world that truth and humor are always a more effective medicine than soothing platitudes and stock business speak. A must read for all leaders and their consultants."

Roger Housden, best-selling author of Ten Poems to Change Your Life and many other books.

"I commend this book of Nasrudin stories to you; it is in fact an entirely commendable book – wiser even than The Hitch Hiker's Guide to the Galaxy, far, far funnier than In Search of Excellence, so much thinner than The Harvard Business Review Encyclopaedia of Corporate Strategy, and astoundingly cheaper than Catch 22!"

Professor Mike Pedler, co-author of the best-selling books The Learning Company and The Manager's Guide to Self-Development.

"We've never had a lasting consensus on what 'leadership' really is. But whatever it is, the

Nasrudin stories apply incredibly well. Every story in this little book is memorable and everyone contains a kernel of wisdom that is worthy of considerable pondering if you are a leader, an aspiring leader, or a leader's coach."

John Adams, Chair, Organizational Systems Program, Saybrook Graduate School, San Francisco, and author of *Transforming Leadership*.

"Any of us who take any kind of leadership does so with unexamined assumptions about what leadership involves. The short stories in this book will challenge and potentially expose your assumptions. Sometimes you will laugh, sometimes you will squirm, sometimes you'll find the story pointless. But will you see the leadership assumptions etched within your own responses?"

Bill Torbert, Professor of Management, Boston College and author of *Action Inquiry: The Secret of Timely and Transforming Leadership*.

The Wise Fool's Guide to Leadership

Short spiritual stories for organizational and personal transformation

Peter Hawkins

BOOKS

Winchester, UK
New York, USA

Copyright ° 2005 O Books
O Books is an imprint of John Hunt Publishing Ltd.,
Deershot Lodge, Park Lane, Ropley, Hants, SO24 OBE, UK
office@johnhunt-publishing.com
www.O-books.net

Distribution in:
UK
Orca Book Services
orders@orcabookservices.co.uk
Tel: 01202 665432 Fax: 01202 666219 Int. code (44)

USA and Canada
NBN
custserv@nbnbooks.com
Tel: 1 800 462 6420 Fax: 1 800 338 4550

Australia
Brumby Books
sales@brumbybooks.com
Tel: 61 3 9761 5535 Fax: 61 3 9761 7095

New Zealand
Peaceful Living
books@peaceful-living.co.nz
Tel: 64 7 57 18105 Fax: 64 7 57 18513

Singapore
STP
davidbuckland@tlp.com.sg
Tel: 65 6276 Fax: 65 6276 7119

South Africa
Alternative Books
altbook@global.co.za
Tel: 27 011 792 7730 Fax: 27 011 972 7787
Text: ° 2005 Peter Hawkins

Design: Jim Weaver
Cover design: Krave Ltd., London
ISBN 1 903816 96 3

All rights reserved. Except for brief quotations in critical articles or
reviews, no part of this book may be reproduced in any manner without
prior written permission from the publishers.
The rights of Peter Hawkins as author have been asserted in accordance
with the Copyright, Designs and Patents Act 1988.

A CIP catalogue record for this book is available from the British
Library.
Printed and bound by CPI Group (UK) Ltd, Croydon, CR0 4YY

Contents

Acknowledgements

I WOULD like to thank the many people who have contributed to making this book a reality. Some have told me stories, others have commented on the many drafts. In particular I would like to thank my good friends Stephen Lustig, Mike Pedler, Judy Ryde, Joan Wilmot and Robin Shohet who have encouraged me to finish the book and made many suggestions about how it could be presented. In particular, Robin has acted like a midwife to this book when I have wanted to give up, out of exhaustion with the birth.

Pauline Allsop, Lesley Bees, Rosie Howarth and Alison Stephenson have been a great help in fitting in support with typing the book in the midst of all the other demands on the Bath Consultancy Group office.

My long standing group of fellow travelers in the wetern academy , John Crook, Malcolm Parlet, Peter Reason and Peter Tatham, have lovingly supported and challenged my continuing inquiry in how to combine the personal and the organizational and the spiritual and psychological.

Also, a big thank you to Mike Pedler, who has written the preface and has been encouraging about the whole enterprise since he first heard me tell Nasrudin stories at the first Learning

Company Conference many years ago.

Judy (my wife) and my three children (Adam, Daniel and Katherine) have been very patient trial audiences for listening to my recounting the Nasrudin stories over many years. They have also tolerated me chuckling away to myself in front of the computer without having me certified!

Finally, I would like to dedicate this book to Murshid Fazal Inayat Khan who, over many years before his death, taught me to recognize the spiritual in the ordinary everyday world and initiated my love of the many Sufi traditions and living practices.

Peter Hawkins
2005

Preface

THERE was a time, it is said, when all Kings kept fools. While the fool's role was to entertain or cheer up the miserable monarch, it also provided an opportunity for those who dared to "speak truth to power". Protected by the motley and the harlequinade, the wise fool could slip in a bit of straight feedback between the gags.

Peter Hawkins has cunningly chosen the most appropriate modern context for Nasrudin by making him a management consultant. As such, much of his fooling is to do with teaching managers the difference between cleverness and wisdom. However, if this was all Nasrudin did he would soon become a tiresome smart-arse. The wise fool Nasrudin has many aspects to his clowning, of which I like the childlike wonder and openness to the world most, which allows him both to play the fool and to take himself seriously.

One of my favorite stories (told here in a somewhat different guise) takes place as the wise and foolish Nasrudin walks through the town with some of his companions. Along the way they are pestered by children and, on an inspiration, Nasrudin shouts "Children, children, do you know that down at the Town Hall they are giving sweets away?" At this all the children become very excited and run off towards the town square. Nasrudin watches them go, ponders for a moment and then suddenly picks up his skirts and charges after them. His friends are amazed: "What are you doing Nasrudin you fool, you just made that up to get rid of them!" "Ah yes" shouts back the galloping Nasrudin, "but, who knows, it may be true!"

Wouldn't you like to be as free as Nasrudin? Maybe just for your birthday? So much of management these days seems to consist of chasing other people's expensively peddled rainbow dreams of "excellence" or of "being the best" or suchlike. Where success and domination are so prized, we have a great need for wise fools. How can organizational leaders manage wisely and well without a fool to bash them occasionally with the pig's bladder?

Who laughs at (rather than with) Richard Branson and Anita Roddick? Somebody should. Who tells the truth to the Chairmen of Glaxo or Harrods? Only a fool that's clear – and they are thin on the ground within the higher ranks. Does Tony Blair have a fool? (Nominations please on a postcard.) I do hope so. With such a fool, would Sir Geoffrey Boycott not just have been Yorkshire and England's premier opening cricket batsman, but a lovable human being as well?

There is an urgent need for a development program for corporate fools – an MFA perhaps – to strengthen this vital aspect of the financial and mental wellbeing of the western world.

I only know of one senior leader who has a corporate fool. A few years ago, Paul Birch, a senior planner with British Airways, got permission from the then Chief Executive, Colin Marshall, to put "Corporate Jester" on his business card. Paul used to liven things up by challenge and ridicule and by suggesting all sorts of creative new ways of running things; from business meetings, to planning processes, to payment systems. However, the last I heard was that he had retreated to Wales and was working as a consultant!

Back to the Nasrudin. I commend this book of Nasrudin stories to you; it is in fact an entirely commendable book – wiser even than *The Hitch Hiker's Guide to the Galaxy*, far, far funnier than *In Search of Excellence*, so much thinner than *The Harvard Business Review Encyclopedia of Corporate Strategy*, and, astoundingly, cheaper than *Catch 22*!

Professor Mike Pedler

Introduction

Have you ever read a book or been to a talk on leadership and later realized that the one thing you remembered was a story or joke the writer or speaker told? A short story can often speak more profoundly than pages of advice.

For the subject of leadership, I have found story to be even more crucial. Firstly, because leadership is fundamentally about relationship (for leadership to exist there needs to be a minimum of a leader, a follower and a shared endeavor) and story is the language of relationship.

Secondly, to develop leadership is less about learning new skills and more about unlearning habits and breaking free from limiting mindsets we have already acquired.

I was once asked by a chief executive for help in learning to tell stories and jokes. "Why is this important?" I asked him.

"Because I need to engage my staff, capture their attention and then encourage them to think in new ways."

"I know just the person that could help you," I told him, "the wise fool Nasrudin."

"Who is Nasrudin?" he asked.

This is the story I told him.

Nasrudin is the wise fool that belongs to every age and is also timeless. Nasrudin stories are universal. He is to be found in many parts of the globe, from the Far East to the west coast of Ireland and beyond, but most notably throughout the Middle East.

Idries Shah, who has published many splendid volumes of the Nasrudin stories, writes:

> Many countries claim Mulla Nasrudin as a native, though few have gone as far as Turkey in exhibiting his grave and holding an annual Nasrudin festival, when people dress up and enact the famous jokes at Eskishehir, the reputed place of his birth.
>
> (Idries Shah 1966)

According to the people of Eskishehir or Aksehir, Mulla Nasrudin is known as Nasreddin Hodja, and was born, the son of an Imam, in the village of Horto in Sivrihisar in 1208, and died in 1284 in Aksehir, where they have both a grave and a mausoleum dedicated to him. However, his life and many stories cannot be contained within history.

Nasrudin is best known in his guise as a Sufi wise fool, but I am aware that his stories turn up in other spiritual traditions that have a sense of humor. There are Zen, Taoist and Christian stories as well as the stories of the Jewish tradition. Nasrudin is the enlightened Master of the market place and belongs to all churches and to none.

I first heard some Nasrudin stories in the early 1970s and started collecting them from various sources, some written and some aural. Later in the seventies when I started to give papers at conferences, I remembered my friend Nasrudin and started to always include one of his stories to liven up my talk. He saved my bacon on many occasions, when my anxiety coupled with a conference weary audience was leaving me marooned on a lonely platform. For the last twenty-five years I have told and retold many of these stories, and like all good stories they have changed and matured with constant retelling, the stories being reshaped by the listening audience.

Many people have come up to me after my talks, or written to me later, to enquire about this strange man Nasrudin whose stories I had told. Nearly all of them wanted to discover where they could find out more. To some of them I gave the list of references I include at the end of this book. To others I just told another story.

When I worked as a psychotherapist I often thought what a great psychotherapist Nasrudin would have been. When I changed to working as an organizational consultant and leadership coach, I realized that this was another suitable vocation for Nasrudin. For what better could a fool do in the late twentieth century than become an organizational consultant! The Kings of old, like King Lear, had their wise fool, who cured them of what William Blake termed "single-eyed vision", by telling them what no other courtier would dare to say. Many are the Chief Executives and leaders whom I have worked with who have needed their fool or court jester. These new powerful rulers of large corporations are like the rest of us in this age, prone to be trapped into thinking that is linear, dualistic and blinkered. They and we often fail to see the patterns that connect the apparent opposites and end up treating symptoms that only make worse the underlying problems. From our limited perspectives we create solutions to yesterday's problems, which become the symptoms of tomorrow's troubles.

Nasrudin can stop us in our tracks, turn us upside down,

and make us refresh our perspective. As he might have said to the busy leader rushing to solve the next problem:

"Don't just do something, sit there and listen."

The stories can be worked with in many ways. They are used to shock us into seeing situations and ideas that we have become very familiar with, from a different perspective. Nasrudin invites us to embrace paradox and to realize that causality is not a linear process, but emerges from underlying interconnected patterns. Within the Sufi tradition the stories should work at least at three levels:

- the creative jump of humor
- the psychological shift in one's mind-set, and
- the spiritual dimension of releasing us temporarily from our personal fixity of being.

A good Nasrudin story always has an after-taste or a good kickback. The story slips into the house by its engaging good humor, but once inside it can start to re-arrange the furniture and knock new windows through the walls. This can be very releasing if you recognize the prison in which you often live, but very disconcerting if you have grown attached and comfortable in your institutionalized home.

In this book I have collected Nasrudin stories from many sources, old and new, and re-set them in the world of the modern organization and the world of corporate advisors. Even with those stories I have created, I have tried to stay true to the traditional genre and only use stories that work at each of the three levels. Having collected the stories, I have then arranged them to form an alternative unlearning curriculum for leadership development; one based on wisdom not on knowledge; one based on growing our emotional and spiritual capacity, rather than increasing our cleverness; and one that instead of using outward-bound adventures uses inward-bound paradox.

But we should never forget that Nasrudin stories are also there to make us laugh.

"My problem is I never remember jokes," that Chief Executive then told me.

"What you have to realize," I replied, "is that those who tell jokes, do not remember hearing the jokes, but rather remember telling them. Will you promise me that the next joke you hear and want to remember, you will tell to three different people, in three different locations within twenty-four hours?"

He promised, and as far as I know he is still telling stories.

May you enjoy these stories and have fun in re-telling them.

The Wise Fool

"This fellow is wise enough to play the fool;
And to do that well craves a kind of wit:
He must observe their mood on whom he jests,
The quality of persons, and the time,
And like the haggard, check at every feather
That comes before his eye. This is a practice
As full of labour as a wise man's art:
For folly that he wisely shows is fit;
But wise men folly-fall'n, quite taint their wit."

Viola: in *"Twelfth Night or What You Will"* Act
III, Scene I, by William Shakespeare.

There is an old saying that:

> "The wise man learns from others, the fool from his
> own mistakes."

Nasrudin added that:

> "However, a wise fool is generous enough to let others
> learn from his failures."

Which way success: the search for perfection

WHEN I was young I was brought up with the little rhyme:

Good, better, best,
Never let it rest,
Till your good is better,
And your better, best.

This rhyme was part of my schooling in being determined always to do better and to set high standards for myself and others. For many of us this becomes part of a search for perfection. The perfect partner, the perfect job, the perfect chief executive, the perfect leader.

In organizations this can take many forms. Tom Peters wrote a brilliant best-selling book titled "In Search of Excellence", and started a whole movement of searching for "Global best practice", the benchmark organization we can all copy. Since then many writers, such as Hamel and Prahalad and others, have shown how this search can lead to playing "strategic catch-up" with the so-called "Market Leader", only to find when you think you have caught up with them, they have moved on somewhere else.

Another aspect of this search for perfection is expecting our leaders, or ourselves as leaders, to be perfect and bemoaning the fact that they fail to live up to our unrealistic expectations.

I once sat with a top executive team, next to the Chief Executive and turned to his fellow directors and said:

> "I am fed up with you all telling me what is wrong with your Chief Executive. I think you are all playing the game of waiting for the perfect CEO. I have got some bad news for you. In twenty years of consulting I have never met one. You need to recognize that you are all responsible for his weaknesses."

If we want to be a leader, Nasrudin warns us about expecting perfection from ourselves or those that lead us. Instead we need to develop a self-acceptance and a forgiveness of others. Nasrudin stops our rush for perfection and returns us to the now of the journey.

In search of perfection

Nasrudin was helping a company look for a new chief executive. They had tried all the top recruitment and headhunting firms in the country and in desperation turned to Nasrudin.

Over dinner they started to ask him some questions about himself. Having discovered that he was not married, they asked him had he ever come close.

"Indeed yes," he replied. "When I was young I was very keen to marry the perfect wife. I traveled through many lands looking for her. In France I met a beautiful dancer, who was joyful and carefree, but alas had no sense of the spiritual. In Egypt I met a princess who was both beautiful and wise, but sadly we could not communicate. Then finally in India after much searching I found her. She was beautiful, wise and her charm captured the hearts of everybody she met. I felt that I had found the perfect wife."

Nasrudin paused with a long sigh. So one of the senior managers eagerly asked:

"Then did you not marry her, Nasrudin?"

"Alas," sighed Nasrudin, "she was waiting for the perfect husband."

To what end

The board of a large company were working on their mission statement.

"What is your fundamental purpose?" asked Nasrudin.

"Our mission is to create constantly increasing dividends for our shareholders," they declared.

"To what end?" asked Nasrudin.

"So they make increased profits which they will want to reinvest in our company," they said.

"To what end?" asked Nasrudin.

"So they make more profits," they said, becoming somewhat irritated.

"To what end?" asked Nasrudin nonchalantly.

"So they re-invest and make more profits."

Nasrudin pondered this for a while and thanked them for their explanations.

Later that week they had arranged to visit Nasrudin's house to work further on the Mission Statement. They found him in his garden stuffing oats into his donkey.

"What are you doing?" they asked. "You are giving that poor beast so much food that it will not be able to go anywhere."

"But it is not meant to go anywhere," Nasrudin replied. "Its purpose is to produce manure."

"To what end?" they asked.

"Because without it I can not grow enough oats in my small allotment to feed this greedy beast."

How do I progress

An ambitious young manager came to Nasrudin, looking rather anxious.

"What is the matter?" asked Nasrudin kindly.

"How do I make progress in this company, when they have just de-layered and cut out so many levels of management that most of the rungs are missing on my career ladder?"

Nasrudin thought for a while and then said:

"I used to find ladders helpful when I wanted to break into an upstairs bedroom having lost my key. But now I never lock the door and I find that once I am inside the ladder just gets in my way and stops me making progress."

Next?

Nasrudin was invited to a well-known technology company, which he knew had employed nearly every conceivable type of consultant. He was a little aggrieved that he was at the end of the long queue of those that they had consulted, but consoled himself with the thought that some people leave the best to last. He was also curious about why they might now have turned to him, as they had a reputation of using top consultants who sold off-the-peg solutions.

When he arrived they explained to him how they had already acquired: BS 5750, a Charter Mark, Investors in People Award, as well as being an accredited competency centre and they were wondering what was the next stage in their development.

"Sadly I cannot help you," said Nasrudin.

"Why not?" they asked. "We will pay you twice your normal rate."

Nasrudin replied; "Unfortunately, I am not a carpenter, which is what you need to build a bigger trophy cabinet."

In search of fame

Nasrudin had retired to the village where he was born to live out his days in quiet seclusion. However, his fame had spread far and wide and some intrepid tourists came to seek him out.

One day while he was sitting in the village square, a car pulled up and an inquisitive tourist, who could not remember Nasrudin's name, leaned out and asked:

"Have any famous men been born in this village?"

"As far as I am aware," replied Nasrudin, "Only babies are born in this village."

In search of excellence

A group of senior managers came to learn from Nasrudin about excellence. He invited them all to come with him to the local theme park. When they got there he lead them all immediately to the most frightening ride called the "Loggers leap". They were ushered into small boats, which were pulled by a chain along a small channel of water.

They spent the first half of the ride, going up and down in the pitch black. When they got outside into the light they found themselves being slowly pulled up an enormous slope. As they got to the top, their hearts jumped into their mouths, as they saw what was to come. The boats were released from the traction of the climb and went shooting down at enormous speed through the water at the bottom.

They emerged rather white and wet. One of them enquired of Nasrudin what that had to do with excellence.

"You mean you missed it?" He asked. "Did you not enjoy the moment teetering on the top?"

2

What causes what?
Systemic leadership

Another aspect of the search for perfection is the drive to remove errors and solve problems. I have spent many hours in management meetings listening to managers arguing about THE cause of a problem: "Is this poor performance caused by the inadequacy of the team leader or by the lack of training?" or, "To what do we attribute this drop in sales?"

Many managers believe that solving problems is how they earn their salaries and that every problem has a single cause, which if tackled will solve the difficulties. Unfortunately, most organizational problems are far more complicated than that. Reg Revans, the founder of "Action Learning", famously commented that only puzzles have solutions, problems have multiple causes and a variety of ways of approaching them.

Nasrudin challenges our whole sense of lineal and single causality, by attributing outcomes to the most bizarre causes. At the same time he pokes fun at our superstitions and omnipotence, like not walking on cracks in the pavement, or always taking one's lucky mascot to a football game. He invites us to be less certain about what causes what and to begin to think systemically.

Recent research has shown how human beings over attribute causality to human beings and under attribute causality to contextual conditions. Most of us go one stage further and if something is not working in a relationship locate the cause in the other person: "Now look what you have made me do!"

With Nasrudin's help we can stop looking for the cause, and instead explore the complex web of enabling conditions, which support the development of the apparent difficulty.

No escape

When on holiday in Egypt, Nasrudin was rather disturbed to see the three managers from his most unsuccessful consultancy project walking along the road. He could not bear to face them and have them ruin his holiday, so he quickly lay down in the ditch not far from the side of the road and pretended he was dead.

Unfortunately, they saw him and left the road to examine the ditch and asked him what he was doing lying in there.

He looked up at them and said:

"Believe it or not, I am here because of you and you are here because of me."

Business process re-engineering

A company had heard from its competitors that they had managed to cut costs by re-engineering their business processes and removing unnecessary steps. They did not want to be left behind and so called in the Nasrudin to re-engineer them. He was asked to look at the distribution warehouse and after several weeks reported back to the board.

"How can we change the system to remove unnecessary steps?" they asked.

"It is not the system that needs re-engineering," he replied, much to their amazement. "It is your staff."

"How can we do that?" they asked.

"Well for a start you need them all to have much longer legs, so they take fewer steps in the long distances they walk around the warehouse."

The psychological test

Nasrudin was always pleased to hear about other developments in the field and so he went to visit a personal career advisor. The first thing that the advisor did was to subject him to a whole battery of computerized psychological tests. These included picture association tests where the computer produced pictorial graphics and the person being tested had to type in the first thought that came into their heads.

The computer drew a square.

"A marriage bed," typed Nasrudin.

The computer drew a triangle.

"A couple kissing," responded Nasrudin.

The computer drew a circle.

"A couple making love," typed Nasrudin.

Later that day the psychologist told Nasrudin that the tests clearly showed that he was obsessed with sex.

"What me?" exclaimed Nasrudin. "It was your computer that kept drawing the rude pictures."

Unwanted visitors

One day the head of Human Resources found Nasrudin walking all around the perimeter of the office block chanting and waving his hands.

"What are you doing?" inquired the bemused manager.

"Warding off unwanted visitors."

"But we have not had any visitors for over a month," said the manager.

"Ah good," said Nasrudin, "my intervention must be working."

The list

Nasrudin was having a working lunch, in the canteen, with his team of consultants, when they were invaded by a group of managers from other parts of the company. In order to get rid of them he turned to them and said:

"Did you know they are putting up a list of promotions and redundancies outside the boardroom?"

The managers all went running off to discover their fate. Nasrudin returned to the discussions with his team, and then suddenly jumped up and went running after the managers.

"Where are you going?" called out his colleagues. "You only made that up to get rid of them."

"You never know," shouted back Nasrudin, still running, "it may be true."

Saving the environment

Nasrudin was invited to speak at a conference on saving the environment. He was to be the final plenary speaker. He listened attentively, but somewhat puzzled, to all the other presentations.

Eventually it came to the time for him to speak.

"I have spent the last three days impressed by your intellectual erudition and your political fervor," he began, "but I am left confused. When I was invited to speak at this conference I was glad I was speaking last as I thought by then somebody would have enlightened me about who the awful person is whom you are trying to save the environment from."

"On the first day I thought it was the politicians, but when they spoke on day two I thought it was the industrialists, but today when they spoke I thought it was the environmental lobbyists. Perhaps we are all trying to save the environment for ourselves. But has anyone asked the environment whether it wants to be saved?"

Moving from where you are

Nasrudin heard a radio program that reported that the majority of travel accidents happened within two miles of a person's home.

He immediately decided to do something to lessen the risks he was obviously taking, and moved house to live three miles down the road.

It's who you don't know

Nasrudin was asked what was his most important breakthrough in establishing himself as a successful executive.

"Well, when I was starting out I went to the largest conference of influential businessmen that I could find. The Minister of Trade gave the opening address and people were so impressed when we were seen on the television cameras talking together, that everyone offered me work."

"What did you talk to the Minister about?" they enquired.

"I said that I was Mr. Nasrudin and would one day be a very successful leader. He replied, 'Get out of my way, you fool!'"

3

Eating the menu

A LITTLE boy had often watched aeroplanes taking off and climbing high into the sky, from his back garden. It came the time of his first flight in a plane. He braced himself for the take-off and as they started to climb high into the air, he turned to his father and asked, "When do we start to become small?"

Like the little boy, all of us can confuse reality with what we perceive from our limited perspective. Kozybski pointed out how, in our language, we often confuse the map with the territory. Gregory Bateson made this even more graphic when he commented that many of us live our lives like a man who wanders into a restaurant, eats the menu and wonders why he is still hungry. In today's world many of us spend more time collecting cookbooks than cooking; and more time reading books of walks than actually walking. Menus are more predictable, more ordered than the rich chaotic nature of life. Of course I hope this book tastes good! Leadership has many recipes and there are hundreds of maps of the territory.

Maps are very useful, when used in their right place – to study maps at base camp before setting out to climb the mountain, or to check the next stage of the journey is sensible. But to spend one's time looking at the map when you are in a blizzard or deep in the jungle surrounded by animals, is somewhat foolhardy.

Many spiritual traditions instruct us that it is important not to stay looking at the pointing finger, but to look at where the finger is pointing.

Nasrudin interrupts our confusing reality with our perception of it by showing the absurdity of some of our perceptions and confusions.

What is an organisation?

A board of Directors invited Nasrudin to help them change their organization.

"What is this organization that you want me to help you to change?" enquired Nasrudin.

The Chairman produced the glossy company annual report, full of graphs and pictures of Directors shaking hands with the workers.

"So you want me to redesign this report for you?" said Nasrudin, who was always ready to help.

"No, no," interjected the Finance Director, "that is just what we tell the shareholders. Take a look at these company accounts. These will give you the real picture."

Nasrudin flicked through the pages, each full of columns and columns of figures. "So am I to understand that your organization is made up of figures, all neatly lined up in rows on paper?" he enquired.

"Not at all," replied the Operations Director. "Take a look at this organizational structure chart. This will show you how we are put together."

"I see," said Nasrudin, and the board thought that at last they would get some sense from him. "The company is made up of a series of boxes, each joined to the others by straight and dotted lines."

The Human Resources Director said, in exasperation, "All right, the organization is not the propaganda, the accounts or the written structure. I understand the point you are trying to make. Unlike my colleagues, we in HR fully understand that the organization is really the people. If you like I will clear the car park and get all our four thousand employees out there. Then you will really see our organization."

"So," said Nasrudin, "your organization is a large crowd, in an empty place, wondering what the hell they are doing there."

Improving the quality

Nasrudin was carrying out a Quality Audit of a construction company. He was walking around a building site when he noticed a carpenter who was building a fence. As he watched he noticed that the carpenter was discarding half of the nails. Nasrudin rushed across to him and enquired why he was wasting so many nails.

"Well," said the Carpenter, "it is the fault of my supplier. Half of these nails they have given me have the heads on the wrong end."

"Don't you realize?" said the helpful Nasrudin. "Those are for the other side of the fence."

The truth exposed

An undercover journalist from a popular newspaper was keen to expose the fraudulent practices in Management Development and decided that Nasrudin was a good target. He posed as a successful businessman who wanted individual consultancy and personal mentoring. He arranged to visit Nasrudin, who agreed to be his mentor. Nasrudin suggested to him that he come weekly for as long as it took to work through all his personal issues.

Two years later, Nasrudin asked him why he was still coming as he was clearly having difficulty finding issues still to work on. The pretend manager said, "I am glad you consider it time to end, for now I can expose you as an impostor. Everything I have told you in our sessions, I made up and was untrue. This just shows what a charlatan you are."

"I may be a charlatan, but perhaps you are a successful businessman merely masquerading as a journalist. How do you know that your readers do not see through you, to what lies beyond?"

At this the visitor left. He was last reported to be running a very successful company.

How old are you?

Some managers in an organization that Nasrudin had worked with for many years were wondering how old this wise fool now was. One of them plucked up the courage to ask him. He quickly replied:

"Just over forty."

Another manager was shocked at this reply and said:

"But that is the same answer you gave about ten years ago!"

"Well that just goes to show how consistent I am," replied Nasrudin.

Portraying reality

Nasrudin became a famous artist, celebrated for his abstract art. One day he was accosted by a fellow traveler on a railway train, who said:

"You must be the famous artist, Nasrudin."

"I have that honor," he replied.

"Why don't you paint things the way they are in reality?" asked the stranger.

"And how is that?" enquired Nasrudin.

"You know," said the man, "how they actually look."

"I am afraid I do not know what you mean," responded Nasrudin.

"Like this," said the man, pulling out his wallet and extracting a small passport-sized photograph, "this is my wife, the way she actually looks."

"I see," said Nasrudin, taking the photograph in his hand. "She is very small and rather flat."

(This story is drawn from the life of Pablo Picasso, but included here as Picasso was clearly unconsciously under the influence of Nasrudin at the time.)

Chaos theory

Nasrudin was working for a company of consultants who were all keen on applying "Chaos Theory". They gave him a copy of the latest book that showed how chaos theory could predict the unpredictable.

Several weeks later they asked him whether he had read the book.

"No," he replied, "I have done better than that, I have put the theory to the test. I fed the book, page by page to my donkey, and now I am waiting to discover whose chaotic behavior improves first, my own, the donkey's, or you the consultants. Meanwhile I am starting a "book" on the outcome and you are all welcome to place your bets."

Changing the culture

Nasrudin was meeting with the Board of a large company. They asked him to tell them how they could change their organizational culture.

"What do you really want to change?" he asked.

"The Mission Statement, the company logo, our rituals etc." replied the first.

"You sound like a faded film star who is trying to regain her popularity by having plastic surgery," Nasrudin said.

"No, no," said the second, "we want to change our behavior, how we relate to the workers on the factory floor. We want them to understand us."

"It sounds as if the faded film star wants elocution lessons," was Nasrudin's laconic reply.

"My colleagues do not understand," interjected the third. "It goes much deeper than they realize. We need to change our mind-sets, the perspectives through which we look at issues."

"The old film star needs new spectacles?"

"That is unfair," broke in the fourth, "what we need to get

to the bottom of is how it feels working in the company, the motivations that underpin our collective being together."

"Ah!" replied Nasrudin, "I see the fading film star has finally decided that it is time for psychotherapy. However, she is still a fading film star."

4

Don't trust the packaging

MANY companies believe they have a vision because they have a vision statement or a great strategy because of the length of their strategic plan document. Many consultants are hired on the basis of their ability to make great presentations, not on their ability to deliver the project. However, the presentation is not the same as that which is referred to by the presentation, the wrapping is not the goods.

In our western consumer society, we can become obsessed by presentation and packaging. We can judge people by what they wear, or worse, the brand name on their clothes. We package to impress and care more about showing off the china and smart wine at the dinner party than attending to our guests.

As a consultant, Nasrudin plays the packaging game and then debunks the charade in such a way that catches us admiring the wrapping not looking at the goods, impressed by the presentation and not questioning what lies beyond it.

Packaging spirituality

Nasrudin attended a conference on Spirituality in Organizations. He was walking through the bar when he heard a group of managers discussing the difficulties they had with spirituality in their organizations. Being both interested in the subject and rather nosy, he stopped to listen.

"The packaging and promotions department have real problems with spirituality," complained one of them, rather pretentiously.

Nasrudin stopped and said, "Ah, my friends, but have you considered the problems that spirituality has with your packaging and promotions department?"

What is a management consultant?

Nasrudin was asked for a definition of a Management Consultant. He replied:

"A consultant is someone who when you ask them what is the time, will first borrow your watch, tell you the time and then charge you for the service. And if you are not careful he will keep your watch."

Noticing the uncomfortable look of recognition on those enquiring, he continued:

"From your looks it would seem to me that you have suffered this plight and lost your watches. Do not worry, I have several here that I can sell you."

Mission statements

The senior management team had spent two days in a hotel creating their new "Mission Statement". They were now anxious to issue it to all the staff on high-quality glossy paper.

"I would recommend that you use cheap paper and make it in the shape of a paper airplane," interjected Nasrudin.

The managers were all rather perplexed and asked him to explain himself.

"It will increase productivity by saving the staff time when they receive their copies."

Buying the packaging

Nasrudin was invited to make a presentation to the board of a prestigious City firm, as part of a competitive tender for a large consultancy assignment. A week later he was told that he had failed to be awarded the contract despite the fact that he clearly had the best insight into the company and the best designed process for bringing about the required change.

"You see," said the Human Resources Director, when offering him the feedback on his pitch, "I am afraid that your whole presentation style was just not smart enough. You should have worn an expensive suit, and used well-produced slides rather than that rather crumpled flip chart. Some smart brochures would also have helped."

Six months later the City firm re-contacted him to say that the consultants who had been awarded the contract had not turned out to be as good as their presentation suggested, and had recently been fired. Nasrudin was asked if he would come back and present his thinking again, but this time would he please remember to wear his best suit.

Always wanting to oblige, Nasrudin came back to the board, dressed in a new black pinstriped suit and with all his ideas presented in a well-designed PowerPoint slide show. Nasrudin presented each member of the board with copies of all the slides in a very glossy brochure. He was duly offered the contract.

The day arrived when Nasrudin was to turn up for the first day of his assignment. The board of the City firm were rather shocked when he failed to turn up and instead a taxi arrived with a large box from Nasrudin.

The Human Resources Director rang Nasrudin to find out what was going on. Nasrudin said:

"Why were you expecting me? You made it quite clear that you did not want to employ me. If you open the box you will find the one you employed."

The Director put down the phone and went and opened the box. Inside he found Nasrudin's new suit, PowerPoint slides and glossy brochure."

The Nasrudin conference

Nasrudin became so famous that his followers organized an international conference of Nasrudin stories. At the conference many stories were told and many learned papers were given on such subjects as "storytelling and spirituality", "storytelling and transformation", "storytelling and humor" and "stories in organizations".

Nasrudin was asked what he thought about the conference that was giving such international acclaim to his stories. He replied:

"I don't suppose it will do much harm."

The forgotten head

Nasrudin was trying to get a contract with a new client company. He would regularly turn up at the company headquarters hoping to speak to the Chief Executive.

One day when he was about to enter the building he noticed the Chief Executive looking out of the window of his top floor office. On arriving at the Chief Executive's office he was told by the secretary that the Chief Executive had gone out for the morning.

"Please can you inform your boss," Nasrudin politely said, "that when he goes out he should remember to take his head with him."

5

Neither this nor that: beyond dualistic leadership

A FTER many years of attending executive and management meetings in a wide variety of organizations, I decided the biggest waste of time in such meetings was "either-or debates". Every organization seemed to have its own version. For some it was, "Should we grow organically or by acquisition?" For others it was, "Should we centralize or de-centralize?" or, "Should we structure our organization based on product, geography or customer type?"

From this experience I drew up what I gradually called "the law of either-or", which reads, "If you are having the same either-or debate for the third time, you are asking the wrong question." Building on the work of others, such as Charles Hampden-Turner (1990), I developed ways of working with such organizational dilemmas. This involved acknowledging the rightness of the need represented by both parties, while pointing out that both their solutions, by the context of the debate, had to be inadequate and incomplete. The only way forward was to find a new solution that had not yet been conceived, and one that met both the needs currently polarized.

Later I discovered that this approach had an ancient lineage. It can be found in the Indian approach of "neti-neti", neither this nor that; in the Socratic dialogues of ancient Greece; and in Hegelian dialectics. It can also be found in the Christian notion of "righteousness" which originally meant to have the ability to stand balanced, embracing both opposites.

Nasrudin may be a fool, but he is also a righteous man who can embrace both sides of an either-or debate and understand the dynamic relationship between the opposing elements. He can also point the way to move beyond dualistic leadership.

In his book *The Contrarion's Guide to Leadership* (2002), Steven Sample recommends that leaders need to develop what he terms "gray thinking" the ability to understand the subtle shades of possibility in an issue rather than just the polarized opposites. Others argue for replacing "either-or" thinking with "both-and" thinking. Although I agree with both these recommendations, I believe they still leave us caught in dualistic thinking. To go further we need to "embrace the opposites", holding the creative tension until, from their relationship, a new possibility emerges that transcends the dualistic frame. Nasrudin once pointed out that to understand 1 and 1 = 2, you need to not only understand the nature of the numbers, but also the nature of "and".

Bill Torbert (2004) has shown that there is an increasing need for Leaders who can embrace paradox and work with more than one reality in play at the same time. He and his associates have researched the dominant frame of thinking of many leaders in organizations both in America and Europe and have found that only a small percentage are coming from what he terms the leadership level of the "strategist-integrator". When individuals have achieved this level of development they are much more comfortable with engaging with contradictory realities and understanding each within their own frame of reference. This makes them more able to work with conflict, without taking sides and instead focus on finding a higher-order resolution.

Not all successful leaders need to come from this level of development. However, in working with Tolbert's ideas, we have come to the conclusion that organizations with three or more dimensions of matrix or a complexity of stakeholders, partnerships or alliances, need to have some leaders who can operate from this level. Also that an organizational transformation process that shifts not only the strategy but also the culture of an organization, needs leadership from this level of development.

In watching such leaders in action, we notice them connect what is being talked about in the future with what is happening in the room right now. We hear them translate one person's worldview to make it understandable to others who come from very different frames of reference. We see them inquiring into and exploring new propositions, rather than debating from a fixed oppositional position. We notice the leader using paradox and humor to make unusual connections and shift people's mindsets and emotions.

Very few people do this work instinctively. Most of us have to learn. One way to learn is to ask Nasrudin to be your mentor.

The Sun or the Moon

Nasrudin was asked which was more important, the Sun or the Moon. To everyone's surprise, he said that he thought that it was obvious that the Moon was more important. Several of those present, started to question him and asked him to explain why.

"Well, the Sun only shines by day, when we have plenty of light to see by, but the Moon helps us to see in the dark."

The internal grievance

Nasrudin was asked to mediate an internal grievance between a boss and his subordinate. After listening attentively to the subordinate lay out his case for being badly treated by his boss, he was much moved and said:

"You are surely right."

The boss, somewhat indignant, put his case for how he had tried absolutely everything to get the subordinate to perform and it was only by being harsh that he could get any response. Nasrudin was much taken by his logic and declared:

"You too are surely right."

By this time the Director of Human Resources was both perplexed and angry, and remonstrated with Nasrudin.

"Mr. Nasrudin, what kind of judgment have you made? You have said that both of the men are right. For real justice you need to decide which is guilty?"

"Yes," replied Nasrudin, "you are right too."

Restructuring

A medium sized company had called in three consultants to help them restructure the organization. The problem was that none of them could agree on whether to restructure on the basis of function, geography or type of customer, or how many management tiers there should be, or how many functional divisions. Nasrudin was called in to help resolve the conflict. Having heard at length the speeches, each arguing for their brilliant solutions, he thought for a while. Then he asked for a large cake and a carving knife.

The consultants and board members looked on with astonishment as he cut the cake first into segments and then tried slicing it horizontally and then diagonally. Eventually he looked up from his very messy plate and said:

"I am sorry to conclude that if you adopt all these plans you are going to end up with lots of crumbs and a good deal of mess."

Which side of the border?

Nasrudin was once a managing director in an international manufacturing company. He was head of a factory in Russia on the border with Finland. All was well until the two countries began the process of once more redrawing the boundary between their two territories. Both countries wanted the factory to be on their side of the border.

Eventually they asked Nasrudin which side of the border he believed the factory should be located.

"Finland." He said without hesitation.

"Why is that?" asked the dismayed Russian official.

Nasrudin replied: "My staff and I could not bear any more cold Russian winters."

6

Identity

MANY of us spend much of our lives, trying to discover ourselves, to find out who we really are? In particular, in recent years in the so-called "developed west", there has been an enormous upsurge in self-development workshops, conferences, books and films. Some of these come from a psychological perspective, some from spiritual perspectives. Having worked much of my life in these fields, I have become more aware of the paradox, that the more I go searching for myself, the less I am able to find it. This paradox is embraced by many of the subtle religions, which talk of how the one we are seeking is the one that is doing the searching, and how the eye cannot see itself.

In the Christian Bible it speaks of how the only ones who find themselves are the ones who are willing to lose themselves. The more we cling to our notion of the self, the more we become alienated and separated from our true self.

I was reminded of this recently when talking with an organizational consultant, who was wondering why, despite the brilliance of their organizational insight and depth of experience, they did not get as much work as they would like. They asked me for feedback and I told them how I noticed that when they were with a new client, they quickly flagged up their difference in various ways. I pointed out that they would dress differently to the client, ensure the client knew that they had had an unusual background and that they would use very different language. They responded by saying that they thought it was important to assert their difference, in order not to collude with the client organization and anyway it was their difference that the organization most needed. They then said that they thought it was imperative that the consultant held integrity by being true and authentic to themselves. I wondered who or what this "self" was to which we wanted to stay true? Is it the self-contained in how we are described on our business card, or in our often inflated curriculum vitae; or the self we perform in role? I started also to wonder about how, in being authentic to our notion of ourself, it is easy to become inauthentic to being with the other and a barrier to putting ourself in the service of what needs to happen.

Nasrudin, usefully, pokes fun at our sense of self and our fixity of identity. If we let him, he can loosen the bond between me and who I like to think I am, and create the space for new learning to occur.

Can you identify yourself?

Nasrudin went into a bank that he did not usually use and asked to withdraw a large sum of money from his account. The bank clerk was naturally suspicious and asked him politely:

"Have you any means of identifying yourself?"

Nasrudin reached down into the pockets of his long cloak

and found an ornate mirror. He held the mirror up and looked studiously into it and exclaimed to the clerk:

"Yes, that's me all right."

How important are you?

Nasrudin was often short of work and food. One day as he was wandering through a hotel, he noticed a senior corporate team having a delicious meal. He walked in, hoping for a little free food. The only free seat happened to be next to the Chief Executive, so he sat down and tried to look inconspicuous. The Chief Executive turned to him and insisted that he identify himself.

"Are you an important board level consultant?"

"No, I rank above a board level consultant," answered Nasrudin.

"Are you a Chief Executive from another company?"

"No, I outrank a Chief Executive."

"Are you a Chairman in disguise?"

"No, I am above that rank as well."

"Then you must be God," the Chief Executive said sarcastically.

"No, I am above that."

"There is nothing above God!" shouted the Chief Executive.

Nasrudin replied calmly, "Now you know who I am. That 'nothing' is me."

(This story come from my friend the storyteller Kamran Zahabian.)

Leaving his cells behind him

Nasrudin had several friends to stay for a couple of days over the New Year. Over dinner he told them all about a new book he was reading on the "new sciences", which showed how important bacteria had been to the evolutionary processes of this planet. He continued by saying how we each contained whole colonies of different bacteria.

"What is the difference between bacteria and cells?" asked one of the guests.

Another guest replied, "Cells are you, whereas bacteria are not."

Nasrudin was puzzled by this, and even more puzzled when he later read in the same book that on average you shed 100,000 skin cells a day, which accounts for most of the household dust. He anxiously telephoned his friends who had returned to London. He enquired of the wife of the second guest:

"How is your husband, are you sure he is alright?"

"Why are you so concerned?" she replied.

"Because he may not be aware of it, but 200,000 parts of him are still floating around my house."

The center of the universe

There was a heated argument going on in the bar of the hotel about where the centre of the universe resides. Many "experts" were vehemently putting forward their convictions. Someone suggested that they stop and ask Nasrudin who was quietly sitting in the corner, listening to their debate.

"You are old and wise, Nasrudin. Where do you think the centre of the universe is located?"

"That is easy," replied the old teacher quietly. "It is located in the organization that is going to pay me my next check."

The airport bookstall

Nasrudin was waiting for a plane, when he was surprised to see a book on the bookstall, full of stories purporting to be about his life. He started to read it and wandered off still chuckling.

7

The nature of learning

IN western education we so often confuse learning with acquiring data or information. Learning, we are taught, is about memorizing facts and regurgitating them in the correct way to pass exams. "Now, what I want is *facts*. Teach these boys and girls nothing but facts. Facts alone are what is wanted in life," said Dickens' Mr Gradgrind in *Hard Times*.

In this belief, experts are seen as having jugs full of learning, and we go to sit at their feet in the hope that they will pour some of this learning into our empty mugs! Learning is a product you can buy and measure.

Nasrudin pokes fun at this way of seeing learning. He shows us how learning resides in relationship, not individual experts. Also, he illustrates how learning grows out of digested experience, rather than residing in textbooks, as we so often believe.

The Indian poet Kabir catches this notion beautifully when he writes:

"There is nothing but water in your holy pools.
I know, I have been swimming in them.

All the Gods sculpted of wood or ivory can't say a word.
I know, I have been crying out to them.
The Sacred Books of the East are nothing but words.
I looked through their covers one day sideways.
What Kabir talks of is only what he has lived through.
If you have not lived through something, it is not true."

The Kabir Book by Robert Bly 1997

Many organizations embarked with great hope on the quest for Knowledge Management, only to end up with enormous data warehouses, full of well-filed data that was never accessed. A world that was pre-figured by T.S. Eliot, when he wrote:

"Where is the wisdom we have lost in knowledge?
Where is the knowledge we have lost in information?"

(T.S. Eliot *"The Rock"*)

It is important that we understand the difference between the various elements of the knowledge hierarchy.

Wisdom
Understanding
Knowledge
Information
Data

Learning is the process of transforming the lower elements of this hierarchy, to create the higher elements. As an early Sufi poet wrote: "Knowledge without wisdom is like an unlit candle." True learning ultimately involves lighting the wick and setting fire to what we think we know. Nasrudin is a useful arsonist.

Finished learning

An excited father came running up to Nasrudin waving a letter. "I have just heard from my son that he has passed his M.B.A. and finally finished all his learning.

"Console yourself, Sir," began Nasrudin, "I am sure that God in his infinite wisdom will soon send him some more."

There is more light out here

Some of the Nasrudin's consultancy apprentices were assisting him carrying out an audit of the culture of a large organization. They found him wading through a whole desk full of statistical data that had been compiled from extensive psychological tests of all the employees. He was engaged in doing complex analysis of all the interconnecting variables of each of the various psychological types that worked together.

"But Nasrudin!" exclaimed one of the apprentices, "You have taught us many times that the culture of a company does not reside in the psychology of the individuals but in what happens between the individuals and between the various parts of the company and also at the boundary of how the company relates to its stakeholders and environment."

"Very true and well remembered," replied Nasrudin, returning to his immersion in the mountain of files.

"But if that is true, why are you looking for the culture in all these individual psychological scores, gleaned from an examination room and not from what happens in the lived culture?" they asked.

"Ah!" said Nasrudin, "You fail to recognize that there is so much more data here."

Learning from the experts

Nasrudin was asked on another occasion about his own training as an organizational consultant. In response he told this story.

Many years ago I decided to find the quickest way to become rich. A friend of mine told me that the best method was to invest in jade. It must be of the highest quality, he told me, or you will waste your investment. The problem was, how could I learn to distinguish top quality jade from the inferior article?

I decided to search out the finest expert in the area. Everybody I asked mentioned the same highly regarded teacher and so I sought him out.

"Yes, I certainly can teach you to recognize top quality jade," he told me. I asked him how long it would take to learn and he replied, "I can teach you in five days, but it will cost you the equivalent of $10,000 or £5,000."

It seemed a high price, but he was reputed to be the world expert and I presumed I would learn a great deal in those five days, so I agreed to the contract. He told me to come to his house each day between 9 and 10 a.m., starting the next day.

An hour a day seemed a little on the short side for such an expensive training, but I duly turned up the next day and was ushered into a room with a long wooden table. In the middle of the table was a large piece of green stone. Placed either side were two chairs. The Master sat on one side and I was invited to sit on the other.

"Look at the jade," he commanded.

I stared and stared, expecting that at any moment he would start telling me what I should be noticing, but not a word was said until the end of the hour, when he declared, "That is the end of today's lesson, I will see you at 9 a.m. tomorrow."

I felt that I had been short-changed on this first lesson, but was sure that he would tell me tomorrow what I should have noticed.

The next day, at the same time, in the same room, I found myself sitting opposite a new piece of rock. "Look at the jade," the Master once again commanded. My study was intermingled with my growing eagerness and anticipation of what I was going to be told. But not a word came from the lips of the Master, until I was once again told that this was the end of the lesson and he would see me tomorrow.

The third day turned out to be the same as the first two. I rationalized my growing fury by telling myself that this being the acclaimed expert, he was waiting for me to have studied several different pieces of Jade before giving me the lecture on how they all differed. In the rest of the week, surely he would tell me how the colors differed, how to notice the fine-grained textures, the edges of the different sides etc.

However, the fourth day came and went exactly as the others had done before them. A new piece of jade, and an hour's silent study

I arrived at the last lesson on the Friday morning, keyed up with anticipation. Now all was going to be revealed and I was sure that I was going to have to really concentrate to get my £5,000-worth of learning into my head in this one short hour.

I was shocked to find the room exactly the same, with another piece of stone and the same invitation – "Look at the jade."

I looked at the jade with urgent anticipation of the wisdom that surely was shortly to be delivered. After ten minutes I could stand it no longer, my patience had finally run out. I turned to the master and shouted at him:

"I have spent £4,000 so far and another £1,000 today, and

so far you have not taught me anything, only left me to look at different pieces of jade. What is even worse, today you have not even had the courtesy to provide me with a piece of genuine jade."

(This story can be found in the Zen Buddhist tradition and I am grateful to Tony Wheildon, for its inclusion here.)

How did you become so clever?

One day Nasrudin was asked:
"How did you learn to become so clever?"
"It was quite easy," he replied. "I just talked a lot and when I saw people nodding their head in agreement, I wrote down what I had said."

The keynote speech

Nasrudin was an intriguing figure in the field of Organizational Learning and so the committee of the professional association decided to invite him to speak at the next conference.

The chairperson introduced him at length and then he rose to his feet.

"Do you know what I am going to tell you?" he asked.

The audience who were used to audience participation, all shouted "No!"

"Then you are not ready to hear it," he replied, before sitting down.

The committee, who received many complaints from the audience, were outraged. The chairperson said, "We cannot let this scoundrel get the better of us. We must invite him back for the next conference." The committee all agreed with their prestigious chair.

On the day of the conference, all the audience were ready, having heard about the events of the last conference. Nasrudin was introduced, got to his feet and said, "Do you know what I am going to tell you?"

"Yes!" shouted out the primed audience.

"Then you do not need me to tell you," said Nasrudin and calmly sat down.

"This is too much. He should be expelled from the association," they were all saying in the coffee break. But the chairperson was stubborn. "No, we must invite this man back next year as the keynote speaker, then we will sort him out."

The big day arrived and as before Nasrudin got up and asked, "Do you know what I am going to tell you?"

Half the audience cried out, "Yes", the other half, "No", as they had been briefed by the chair.

"Then let those who know tell those that do not," said Nasrudin and left the conference.

Learning must be greater than environmental change

A Managing Director had been reading the Darwinian equation for organizational survival, which states that the organization's learning must be equal to, or greater than, the rate of environmental change or the organization will fail to survive. With some concern he asked Nasrudin:

"Can you help us learn faster than our environment?"

"Well, if you tell me who is awarding the prize," replied Nasrudin, "then I will join in the race."

8

Unlearning: unknowing

THE section on learning ended with the lines:

> As an early Sufi poet wrote: "Knowledge without wisdom is like an unlit candle." True learning ultimately involves lighting the wick and setting fire to what we think we know. Nasrudin is a useful arsonist.

This is the process of unlearning. As a developing child, learning is very crucial in order to be able to understand the society and the world around you, and to develop the skills to survive and prosper independently. The same is true for an early stage organization. However, as the individual or the organization grows to maturity, new learning by itself is inadequate in providing the agility to adapt to the changing environment. This is because we feed new data and information into outdated frameworks and assumptions, some of which we have become very attached to, because of the time and effort we have invested in previously learning them. Also, many of the frameworks have become second nature to us, and dropped out of conscious awareness.

Having given the keynote address at the first British conference on "The Learning Company", advocating the importance of the learning organization, I returned nearly ten years later to give another keynote address, in which I warned of the dangers of becoming addicted to learning and the importance of unlearning. I pointed out how little our acquisitive society had written about unlearning as opposed to the hundreds of new books and papers on organizational learning, but I had found a couple of authors and quoted their definitions of unlearning.

Bo Hedberg defines unlearning as:

"... the process through which learners discard knowledge."

He goes on to say:

"Very little is known about how organizational unlearning differs from that of individuals."

But his work explores how unlearning can be blocked, particularly by the danger of too much success:

"Organizations which have been poisoned by their own success are often unable to unlearn obsolete knowledge in spite of strong disconfirmations."

March and Olsen (1976), also state that:

"There are times when organizations should treat their memories as enemies."

I would add to these quotes my own definition that:

> "Unlearning is the process by which organizations unlock the evolving of their culture."

But the understanding of the importance of unlearning has been a key part of many spiritual traditions and in the paper I quoted several great spiritual teachers: first Krishnamurti (1954), the Indian philosopher, spiritual teacher and mentor of David Bohm:

> Can you think of something that is not knowable? You can only think of something that you know. But there is an extraordinary perversion taking place in the world at the present time. We think we shall understand if we have more information, more books, more facts, more printed matter.
>
> Obviously, knowledge and learning are an impediment to the understanding of the new, the timeless, the eternal.
>
> With most of us, knowledge and learning have become an addiction and we think that through knowing we shall become creative.

Then Hazrat Inayat Khan (1972):

> The process of spiritual attainment is through unlearning.
>
> People have made their belief rigid ... they are worse because they have nailed their feet to their belief.
>
> Among a hundred persons who come for spiritual guidance, ninety come out of that trap ... They do not

want to give up their own idea, but they want to have it confirmed that the idea they have is right.

Spiritual attainment, from beginning to end, is unlearning what one has learnt. But how does one unlearn? What one has learnt is in oneself. One can do it by becoming wiser. The wiser one becomes, the more one is able to contradict one's own ideas. The less wisdom one has, the more one holds to one's ideas. In the wisest person there is the willingness to submit to others. And the most foolish person is always ready to stand firm to support his own ideas.

Nasrudin uses humor and the unexpected to loosen our bonds to our false certainty and to encourage us to unlearn and create new space for wisdom to enter.

Where are you going?

While working for a top security defense firm, Nasrudin always went for a walk at 12.45 p.m. After a few days the firm's security staff became suspicious. So one day he was accosted by the head of security and asked where he was going.

"I have no idea," he replied.

This made the security chief even more suspicious.

"Don't give me that line," he began. "You always go off somewhere at 12:45, so you better tell me where you are going."

Nasrudin opened his hands in innocent ignorance and said, "I really have no idea."

The security chief knew only one way to deal with this impertinence. He took Nasrudin down to their offices and had him locked up while he called the police.

When the security chief returned with the police officer and entered the locked room, they accused Nasrudin of failing to report where he was going and lying that "He had no idea where he was going."

Nasrudin looked up and said:

"But I really did have no idea that where I was going was to this office prison."

The biggest sin

Nasrudin was conducting a seminar for chief executives on ethical values. The group participants were encouraged to reflect on their personal histories and relate times when they had acted unethically. The first chief executive related how he once had an affair with his colleague's wife. The second dismissively retorted:

"Oh that is a minor ethical lapse, I have done far worse. I lied to the board and shareholders about our company's performance in order to keep my job."

The next leader rose to the challenge:

"The odd lie to the board, I consider par for the course. My ethical failing was greater than both of yours. When I left my previous company I stole all the main clients, in order to start my own business."

The fourth went one better and related how he had regularly stolen money from his company and so it continued. Only Nasrudin had failed to share anything. They finally turned and asked him:

"So what are your ethical sins?"

"My sin is greater than all of yours," he replied.

"What have you done?" they eagerly asked.

"It's not what I have done," he replied, "but what I am going to do. You see I am a compulsive gossip, and I can not wait to get home and tell everybody what I have heard this afternoon."

The cup is too full

One day an eminent consultant and author came and asked Nasrudin whether he would be willing to be his mentor.

"There is nothing I can teach you," responded Nasrudin.

"Don't be so modest," replied the eminent consultant. "I am told that you are the best teacher for somebody like myself who is already an expert in their field."

Nasrudin shrugged and invited the consultant for some tea. He carefully laid the table, brought out his best china and warmed the teapot. When the tea was made he began to pour and kept pouring until the tea was flowing over the edge of the cup and all over the table. Eventually the consultant jumped to his feet and said:

"Stop pouring you fool, can't you see the cup is too full to have any more tea in it?"

"Ah!" said Nasrudin, "I can see that I must empty the cup before I pour any more in, but cups are easier to empty than successful consultants."

Anything you need?

When working away from home with a group of managers, Nasrudin was asked one lunchtime:

"We are going to the shops, is there anything you need?"

"Yes," replied Nasrudin.

"What is it?"
"A haircut."

Palace or hotel?

Nasrudin was weary from a long journey and was looking for a hotel when he saw the entrance of the King's palace. He walked straight in, past the guards, and into a secluded garden where, by chance, the King happened to be having a stroll in the cool evening breeze.

"May I have a room for the night, please?" asked Nasrudin.

"This is not a hotel, this is my palace," replied the King, surprised.

"Who lived here before you?" asked Nasrudin.

"My father," said the King.

"And before that?" asked Nasrudin.

"Well, my grandfather," said the King.

"So, in a place where people come and go regularly like that, how can you pretend that this is not a hotel?"

(This story comes from my friend the storyteller Kamran Zahabian.)

Who is the idiot?

When Nasrudin grew old he retired to a small village in the mountains. Each day he would sit in the village square and watch the world go by.

One day a large American car drove into the village and stopped by where Nasrudin was sitting. The window opened and the American in a large booming voice asked:

"Do you know the way to Vienna?"

"I have no idea," replied old Nasrudin.

"Well, can you tell me the way over these mountains?"

Once again Nasrudin replied, "I have no idea."

The American was getting impatient and shouted, "Well, can you at least tell me the way out of this village?"

"I have no idea," answered Nasrudin.

The American driver angrily asked:

"Are you some kind of idiot?"

Nasrudin calmly replied:

"I may be an idiot, but at least it's not me that is lost."

9

The value of failure

"WHAT has been your best failure?"
I shall never forget the shock of when I was asked this question in an interview. I was prepared to speak eloquently about all my successes, but failure was something I had learnt to sweep under the carpet and to hide, deny or ignore.

I had not yet learnt from Nasrudin that failure is a rich compost for the growth of new learning. Nor had I yet learnt from Gregory Bateson (1973), who points out that all learning is "stochastic", which means that it emerges from trial and error. Yet so much of our western beliefs are based on trying to have trials without errors.

One organization that I worked for were brilliant at strategically analyzing how they should change. They were also brilliant at designing a change process that meticulously included all the necessary elements. However, when it came to piloting the change process, the culture was such that those carrying out the pilot project knew implicitly that they were supposed to demonstrate that everything worked perfectly, with zero errors. They invariably had successful pilots, but with zero learning. Later, when they were in the middle of full implementation, they would encounter the inevitable resistance and problems, for which the pilot process had left them unprepared. At this point they would decide that it must have been the wrong analysis or change design and would retreat to their areas of comfort and skill, namely analysis and change design!

In another organization, after a rather difficult conference, where we had helped launch a new change initiative, I was taken aside and sternly informed; "You are only allowed to fail once around here." This was clearly my final warning after only four weeks of involvement with the organization. I replied, "Well we certainly do have a problem." "What is that?" they asked. "Well I normally fail at least eight or nine times before discovering the best way to work with an organization, and I am not sure how we are going to create the space for that to happen."

I was deliberately underestimating, as Edison, when asked whether he was disappointed to have had so many failures before discovering the light bulb, replied that he had not had ninety-nine failures, just ninety-nine discoveries of how not to make a light bulb. The organizational law of failure is:

"Failure is essential, but it is important to ensure that the value of the learning that ensues is greater than the cost of the failure."

Success

Nasrudin was at a conference with other management consultants. The others were all staying at the most expensive hotel and going out each evening to the best restaurants in town. Nasrudin was sitting in the conference hall eating his plain bread and cheese.

One of his colleagues came up to him and said:

"If only you would learn to tell the companies what they want to hear and were less confrontational, then you would earn better fees and would not have to be left here eating plain bread and cheese."

Nasrudin replied, "If you would learn to live on bread and cheese then you would not have to spend your time telling companies what you think they want to hear."

Fame and failure

Nasrudin published a number of successful books. He was asked at one of his book signings how he had discovered the art of writing. He replied:

"I just started to write, and it was not until my third book that I discovered I had no talent for writing."

"So did you then stop and do something different?" the questioner asked.

"Oh no," responded Nasrudin, "by that time I was far too famous to change track."

Right first time

Nasrudin was invited to attend a major company program to improve quality. As he walked down the corridor to visit one of the program workshops he could hear people chanting: "RIGHT FIRST TIME – EVERY TIME – WITH ZERO DEFECTS."

Nasrudin turned to his host and said:

"How sad that this group have been deprived of the food of failure, but I am sure that God will notice their deprivation and send them some more."

A fine tip

When Nasrudin lived in a small town, he was known by most of the inhabitants. One day he returned to his car to find that the young parking meter woman had just put a parking fine ticket on his car.

He quickly ran after her, shook her warmly by the hand and immediately paid the fine plus a ten per cent tip.

The parking attendant was rather taken aback. At first she thought he was trying to bribe her, but then realized he had also paid the fine. She tried to give him back the tip and explain that this was totally unnecessary. Nasrudin replied in a very loud voice:

"No I insist you take the tip for yourself. As a citizen of this town I am so pleased to see you doing your job so well, and you were very right and proper to put that fine on my car window."

The young woman was becoming embarrassed, as a small crowd was starting to gather. She raised herself up and said in a firm loud voice:

"Mr. Nasrudin, it is not right that you give me extra money. Please just pay your fine and we can leave it at that."

Thrusting the money back into her hands and speaking even more loudly, Nasrudin made a speech about how good she was at her job and it was important that people should recognize her.

Eventually, the young parking attendant could stand it no longer, and slipped away with the extra money, leaving the crowd praising Nasrudin for his generosity.

When the other parking attendants heard about this bizarre and embarrassing episode, they all decided that they would avoid it happening with them. From that day on, whenever any of the attendants saw his car parked beyond its time limit as it frequently was, they would quickly move away.

Needless to say, Nasrudin saved a fortune in fines.

(This story comes from my German colleague Amelie Winhard-Stuart, and is based on her father, who without knowing it, was a follower of Nasrudin.)

10

Leadership development

THE last section focused on the importance of failure to the process of learning and development and now we move on to other aspects of Leadership Development. I used to believe that great leaders were those who managed somehow to avoid failure. As I encountered more great leaders and heard and read about their lives, I discovered that they often have more failures than the average person. What seems to distinguish them is their ability to face the failure, harvest the learning, dust themselves off, and, engage with the next phase of their life.

Much has been written about leadership. Indeed, Warren Bennis, himself a very successful writer on leadership, commented that leadership was the third best selling subject after sex and food! Much of what has been written has emphasized the heroic leader, leading from the top and turning around the organization. More recently, we are seeing a healthy shift in writing in this area – one that recognizes "Leading Quietly" (Badaracco 2002), "Collective Leadership" (Bennis 1996) and that leadership exists at all levels of an organization.

Also, that leadership exists in the relationship between leaders and followers, and that followers, leaders, and a shared endeavor are all necessary ingredients for successful leadership.

Of all the great one-liners on leadership, the one I have found to have the biggest impact on my own learning is:

> "Taking on leadership involves giving up the right to blame others or make excuses."

Leadership is an attitude, a way of approaching life where one is not asking, "how can I succeed?" but "what can I best contribute to this situation?" and "How can I align to what is needed, and what is the difference I can make?"

One of the key tasks of leaders is to develop other leaders. Nasrudin not only challenges us as leaders to take responsibility and to "walk our talk", but to realize we develop other leaders best through what we model. He also helps us to recognize how often our assumptions about ourselves as leaders are often very separate and different from what we expect from those who lead us.

Giving up coffee

A senior manager came to Nasrudin for some individual counseling and pleaded with him to help him give up coffee, because he was drinking it constantly throughout his working day.

After some consideration, Nasrudin told him that he thought he could help him. He asked him to come back and see him in two months' time.

The manager agreed to this appointment and duly returned

two months later.

Nasrudin looked him in the eye and said:

"Stop drinking coffee, you do not need it any more."

The Manger was a little taken aback. "Is that all?" he enquired incredulously.

"Yes," replied Nasrudin, "you will find that your craving for coffee has completely gone."

"Well you could have said that to me when we first met, so why did I have to wait two months and come back and see you?"

Nasrudin smiled and replied, "I had to give up coffee first."

Empowerment

"How can I empower my staff?" asked a chief executive at a seminar that Nasrudin was running in an expensive hotel.

Nasrudin looked him in the eye and asked:

"How did you empower yourself?"

The chief executive was a little unsure how to answer this question, but his years of experience of being on platforms and always having an answer, meant that he was not going to be outwitted now.

"I suppose when I was a middle manager, I got so frustrated with how the senior management were running things I became determined that I could do it better. So I set about demonstrating to whoever would notice that I could do a better job. Eventually they promoted me."

"Well," replied Nasrudin, "tell me, now the roles are reversed, which is it? Are you not frustrating them enough, or do you not notice when they are trying to show you that they can do the job better than you?"

Leadership training

Nasrudin was involved in a discussion about how to develop successful leaders. One person argued that great leaders were born not made, another that a leader was formed by the person being in the right place at the right time. Eventually Nasrudin was asked for his opinion. He replied:

"Recent evidence of successful leaders in politics and business organizations, suggests that a leader becomes great, not by being in the right place at the right time, but by avoiding being in the wrong place at the wrong time."

Alignment

The company had worked hard on its Vision, Core Values and Strategy statements, but the senior executives were having difficulty getting the staff aligned behind the new direction. They consulted Nasrudin and asked him:

"What is the quickest way to get all the company's employees going in the same direction?"

"Just pay me ten times my normal fee and I will complete the task in the next ten minutes," he quickly replied.

They were so impressed that they willingly paid him this outrageous fee, and he immediately left the room and went down the lift. As he walked through the entrance lobby he smashed the fire alarm and shouted "Fire" as loud as he could. Within seconds all the staff were running in the same direction towards the fire exit.

How to get on in the corporation

Several ambitious young managers who aspired to leadership went to see the wise old Nasrudin to obtain his advice on how to get to the top.

"Well," reflected Nasrudin, "when I was young I believed that the people at the top got there because of the inequities of the system – who they knew, what school they had been to, who they kept in with etc.

When I started to ascend the corporate ladder myself I began to discover that those at the top had got there by merit and hard work.

Finally when I got to the top of the organization I realized that those of us at the top got there by chance."

"So what should we do, Nasrudin?" they asked somewhat confused.

"In your case, I think you should check your contacts," he replied.

(This story is based on an interview with the great writer and thinker E.F.Schumacher.)

Leadership communication

MANY organizational leaders fail to understand the difference between information and communication. Often I have heard staff in an organization complain about the lack of communication on the strategic direction, only for senior leaders to respond by saying that they have sent out lots of e-mails and written communication, and the staff are at fault for not reading it. Organizational leaders often develop internal communication policies and talk about the need to send out a communication, without being clear about the difference between information and communication.

In our work we define the difference between information and communication as:

Information	Communication
One way	Two way
Conveying data and facts	Involves data, perspectives and feelings
Involves speaking or writing	Involves listening

Nasrudin challenges us not to confuse these two processes and to consider how to engage in real communication and dialogue.

Dialogue is fundamentally different from either debate or discussion. Peter Senge (1990) points out that the word discussion comes from the same route as the words percussion and concussion, and can often be the equivalent of knocking the other person over the head with your ideas!

In dialogue, all those contributing are trying to discover new meaning and understanding through their mutual exchange. As physicist David Bohm (1996) said, in dialogue we are engaged in collective new thinking, not exchanging pre-cooked thoughts. Our current western society is inundated with information and debate but sadly, true dialogue and communication are very rare.

"Bon Appetit"

Nasrudin soon became rich on his earnings as a renowned management consultant and like many rich fools, decided to go on a cruise. The first night of the voyage he was given a table with a Frenchman. At the beginning of the meal the Frenchman greeted him with "Bon Appetit". Nasrudin thought that the Frenchman was politely introducing himself, so he responded by saying "Mulla Nasrudin". They had a pleasant meal.

However, the next morning breakfast started with the same ritual, the Frenchman saying "Bon Appetit" and Nasrudin who now thought the Frenchman must be a little deaf said even more loudly, "MULLA NASRUDIN".

At lunch the same thing happened and by now Nasrudin was getting a little irritated with what he thought must be a very dim-witted Frenchman. Luckily that day he got talking to a fellow passenger who spoke French and was an inter-cultural consultant and coach. He was able to enlighten Nasrudin and tell him that "Bon Appetit" was a polite French greeting, that meant "have a nice meal".

"Ah! Thank you," said the enlightened and relieved Nasrudin. All afternoon he practiced, walking up and down the deck of the boat. That evening he very proudly sat down at dinner, smiled and said to his new French friend, "Bon Appetit".

"Mulla Nasrudin", the Frenchman replied.

Communication policy

A corporate senior management team asked Nasrudin whether or not he could prepare a communication policy for them, so that they could communicate better with all of their six thousand staff.

"Certainly," said Nasrudin, "only first tell me, in communicating with your staff, what is it that you are not hearing?"

Organizational secrets

When working in a large organization, where there was very little trust and large amounts of paranoia, Nasrudin was constantly being asked to listen to secrets that the tellers did not want anyone else to hear.

Eventually when yet another manager asked him whether he could keep a secret, he replied:

"I am afraid I have no space for any at the moment, as I have to begin to protect myself from other people's storage problems."

12

Change leadership

MUCH has been written about the nature of change management, to the extent that there is now a burgeoning industry and academic discipline in this field. But Nasrudin is very useful at showing how many of our endeavors in this area are over heroic and full of hubris. For in many ways the term "managing change" is an oxymoron, or contradiction in terms. You can enable change, facilitate change, unblock change, but rarely manage it.

Just before I first went to work in South Africa, I watched the television documentary on the serial killer Dennis Neilson. I was struck by the awful story of how he lured people back to his flat and then killed and butchered them, flushing the remains in pieces down the toilet. Unfortunately, for him and his neighbors, he lived in an upstairs apartment, and the people downstairs eventually complained about the smell. The plumbing experts, Dynarod, came round, diagnosed where the blockage was occurring and with their rods, fished out the body parts causing the problem. They immediately called the police, who worked out that they had finally located their serial killer.

The policeman who made the arrest said something like:

> As I was waiting for Mr. Neilson to come home from his
> work, I thought to myself, 'This could be tricky, how am I
> going to confront him?' Then I thought, 'I know, a bit of
> humor could come in handy.' When he arrived home, I
> said to him, 'I have come about the drains.' He knew what
> I meant.

I wondered why this gruesome tale had so caught my
imagination, to the extent that I could not stop thinking
about it all the way to South Africa. Then I realized it was for
two reasons. Firstly, I was so impressed by Dynarod, for they
diagnosed where the blockage was and used the minimum
intervention to unblock the system. Many large consultancies
would have come in and said you need a new plumbing system,
and many weeks and much cost later the problem would have
been solved, but in the meantime the furniture would all have
been moved, the carpets and floorboards all taken up, the
decoration ruined and there would have been a lot of knock on
consequences.

The other reason the story gripped my attention was that I
identified with this marvelous policeman. Many times I have
stood in the outer office of a Chief Executive thinking, "This
could be tricky – how can I tell him what is actually beginning
to smell in his organization? Perhaps a little bit of humor would
come in handy!"

I told the story and my connections to it at the South
African conference, and for many it resonated with their own
experiences of trying to manage change.

Nasrudin reminds us that to change anything beyond

ourselves, we have to first start with changing our self and that is the most difficult step in the whole process.

Draining the alligators

When Nasrudin was helping a management team look at how they managed a major change program of the managers said, "It's very hard to drain the swamp when you are up to your neck in alligators."

"My old, one-legged grandfather," replied Nasrudin, "taught me that when draining alligator swamps, to start quietly at the edge and to avoid jumping into the middle of the pond with all your equipment. If you do the alligators either think, 'Oh good, here comes lunch,' or 'Help, I am under attack,' and bite you first."

How does it affect the parsnips?

Nasrudin had carefully outlined his proposals for the company to manage the much-needed improvements in how it organized itself, when the Chief Executive retorted:

"Yes, but this program of yours, does it butter any parsnips?"

"No," replied Nasrudin, "but it does put manure on them."

Which way for success?

At the end of a very long strategic planning meeting, the Chief Executive turned to Nasrudin and said:

"Well you have heard about where we want to go in the next five years, so now tell us which direction we ought to take to get there?"

Nasrudin stroked his beard and pondered this question for quite awhile. He then replied:

"Well, if that is where you want to get to, I would not start from here."

Turning the company around

After a very long meeting in which the board had strategically planned their management of change program, they enquired of Nasrudin how long he thought it would take to turn the company around?

"Well it all depends," Nasrudin began.

"On what?" they asked.

"On how much you are enjoying the view from the way you are presently facing."

Changing the people

The Head of Human Resources of a large retail company was explaining to Nasrudin how successful he had been. He related how he had sacked nearly 2,000 people at the same time as managing to bring about the necessary change in the company's culture.

"You see we took your advice," said the very pleased manager.

"What advice was that?" asked a slightly worried Nasrudin.

"Don't you remember, you told us 'If you cannot change the people, then change the People'?"

"Ah no," replied Nasrudin, "what I actually said was, 'If you cannot change the People, then change the people'."

Who has the problem?

Nasrudin got married to a senior manager in the same company where he was working. One night she was unable to sleep and kept tossing and turning in the bed so much that it was keeping Nasrudin awake.

"For heaven's sake, what is the matter with you?" he asked.

"Well, I should have completed this report for the Managing Director to present to the board tomorrow morning, and I just could not get it done," she replied.

"You stay there," he commanded. Then he went and phoned the Managing Director.

"What the hell are you doing phoning me at this time of night?" the Managing Director shouted down the phone. "Don't you realize that it is two in the morning and I have an important meeting in the morning."

"Yes I know," said Nasrudin, "my wife should have written your report for you to present in the morning and she is unable to do it."

With that he put down the phone and turned to his wife and said, "You go to sleep. Let *him* have the sleepless night."

Retirement

Eventually Nasrudin retired and was sitting with friends looking back on his life.

"When I was young I was a revolutionary and wanted to change the world.

In mid-life I woke up one day and realized that my life was half over and that I had changed no one. So I prayed that I might be given the strength to at least change those close to me.

Alas, now I am old I simply pray each day for the strength to change myself."

Different directions

On another occasion Nasrudin was asked why it was that despite all the best efforts of the senior executives, all the different departments seemed to go in different directions?

"Well that is easy," replied Nasrudin, "if they all headed in the same direction it would upset the balance, and the organization would topple over."

13

Value, values and stewardship

IREMEMBER the shock of meeting a financial investment manager who was very upset because his annual bonus was only half a million dollars. "How can someone complain about a bonus that is far more that most people's salaries?" I asked this man's boss. "What you do not understand," he replied, "is that most of us only know how much we are loved by the number of zeros on our bonus check."

Value has become so linked to money that money has become an end in itself, rather than a means of creating value. We have forgotten how to value, because we act as if value resides in the object or other person, rather than our relationship with the person or object.

When we talk of my job, my business, my house, we turn our relationship with our work and where we live into objects we own. In some work with organizations, a number of people have been reintroducing the ancient concept of stewardship. As a steward of my house, my focus is on looking after the property so that I can pass it on to the next person to live there in a better state than it is at present. The same approach can be very useful when thinking about our current job, or the company or division or team I am responsible for leading. We are all temporary inhabitants of both property and roles and someone will inherit what we leave behind, not only when we die, but when we move on. It is useful to focus on such questions as:

- What do we want to pass on to our successors? and,
- What would we want to receive if we were them?

On a larger scale the issue of where we invest our sense of value and the concept of stewardship is critical in facing the ecological crisis of our age. To shift the focus from "What can I extract from the material world?" to "What kind of world do we as stewards want to pass on to the subsequent generations?" Unless we can more fully shift from the former to the latter question there is a strong chance that there will not be many more subsequent generations to receive our legacy.

Questions

Nasrudin became tired of the number of times on residential programs, he would end up spending his evenings with one manager after another asking him questions they had not asked in the day. Realizing that he was not getting paid for this "overtime", he sat in the corner of the bar and put up a large notice:

Questions answered.
Two questions for £100.

For the first two hours nobody troubled him. Then eventually the most outspoken group member sauntered up to him and said:

"Isn't one hundred pounds a bit expensive?"

"Yes," replied Nasrudin, "and your second question?"

Intellectual property

Two consultants were arguing about the ownership of a new model of organizational development. They became so stuck they called in Nasrudin to facilitate some conflict resolution.

"Who thought of this idea first?" asked Nasrudin.

"I did," they both said immediately.

"Who most developed it?"

"I did," they both said immediately.

"Who cares most about it?"

Nasrudin could discover nothing that would separate their two claims of ownership.

After a period of pondering this dilemma, he proposed the first step in the resolution.

"I want each of you to spend two days teaching me your new system," he instructed.

They each entered this supposed competition with alacrity, believing that the best teacher would demonstrate their ownership claim.

On the fifth day he called the contestants together and asked:

"Do you both agree that I now have got your ideas?"

"Yes," they both replied immediately.

"Well then," said Nasrudin, "the true owner is the first one to get the ideas back out of which ever part of me they are now in."

The customer-supplier chain

One day the head of the training department decided to sit in on one of Nasrudin's management training sessions. As he walked in, he saw Nasrudin standing in a circle with the group of managers and they were passing around a bottle of spirits.

"All right, I will buy this bottle of whisky from you for $15.30 (£8.50)," said Nasrudin to the manager on his right and duly gave him the money. Then turning to the next manager on his left, he began:

"That very good bottle of whisky that I have acquired specially for you, is now ready. By the way it will cost you $15.75 (£8.75)."

The head of training was shocked and horrified. He was about to dismiss Nasrudin on the spot, when he thought he should wait and gather some more evidence, just in case it went to an industrial tribunal. He watched as the bottle went twice around the circle, each person paying more than the previous buyer. The bottle had reached the princely sum of $27 (£15)), when the head of training could stand it no longer.

"What the hell are you up to?" he demanded of Nasrudin.

"Can't you see?" replied the indignant teacher. "I am helping them learn about the customer-supplier chain. So far they have all managed to create added value to this product. Perhaps you would like to buy this very precious bottle for $28.80 (£16)?"

Valuing the meal

Nasrudin took a number of friends to a small new restaurant. The food was very poor and some of it inedible. When it came to paying the bill, his friends were shocked that Nasrudin left a very handsome tip.

The following week he persuaded them to come to the same restaurant with him. Surprisingly the food was much, much better.

At the end of the meal, Nasrudin once again paid, but this time he left the smallest tip possible.

His friends were really bewildered. "Why did you give a large tip after an awful meal and a small tip after such a good one?" they asked.

He replied, "Last week's tip was for this week's meal, and this week's tip is for last week's meal."

In father's footsteps

Nasrudin was working with the professional conference of engineers.

"Why are you an engineer?" one young professional was being asked by a consultant who was the platform speaker.

"Because that is what my father was," replied the newcomer.

"And why was he an engineer?" continued the performer.

"Because his father was an engineer too."

"So tell me what you would have become if your father and father's father had both been idiots?" quipped the speaker, causing much merriment in the audience.

The young engineer looked trapped and abashed, when Nasrudin who thought he knew the right answer, helpfully shouted out on his behalf:

"A consultant."

In whose time?

When the Nasrudin was a young manager he was always getting into trouble. One day he was called into see his boss, who asked him where he had been all morning. The young Nasrudin replied:

"I had to go and have my haircut."

"You can't do that in work time," replied the indignant manager.

"But I grew the hair at work," said Nasrudin.

"Not all of it."

"But I didn't have it all cut off!"

Fair exchange

Nasrudin decide he needed some new clothes for an important new assignment. He went to a large clothes store and the customer-trained staff patiently served him while he deliberated long and hard about the many alternatives. Eventually, he tried on some very smart trousers. He emerged from the changing room wearing them and asked how much they would cost. On being told that they cost $630 (£350), he immediately took them off in the middle of the store and asked to swap them for one of the suits that only cost $540 (£300).

"But sir," the shop assistant interjected, "you have not paid for the trousers."

"You don't expect me to pay for trousers I don't want, do you?" retorted Nasrudin.

14
Stress for health

THE British Army discovered "shell shock", the US Army "battle fatigue" and modern organizational psychology "stress" and "burn-out". Stress has become fashionable. Some wear it like a badge to demonstrate how hard they work and how important and in demand they are. Others invest a lot of time, money and energy to deal with it.

Without stress you are not alive and we need a certain amount of stress to be awake and responding to the world around us. Other types of stress are a by-product of our way of facing reality or perceiving the world – the stress of thinking I am stressed.

Stress can so easily become nominalized as an object we possess and want to get rid of, rather than seen as a process of engagement or a way of responding to our environment. Stress is a part of life, but we all have choice on how we respond to experiencing it.

Nasrudin encourages us neither to avoid stress nor get stressed worrying about stress. He also encourages the importance of empty time when we can provide the space for new awareness, and creativity to enter. In his own simple way he predates the sentiments of Tom DeMarco, in his recent book (2002) *Slack: Getting Past Burnout, Busywork and the Myth of Total Efficiency*. In this book DeMarco writes:

> Constant overtime and aggressive schedules are symptomatic of the "Hurry Up" organization. Efficiency is pitted against effectiveness, minimizing cost against minimizing time...
>
> What gets lost in this "Hurry-Up" organization is the time it takes to think up new procedures or products; in other words, slack. In today's knowledge-based economy, unlike the factory-based model of prior centuries, creative management of slack is essential for a healthy, growing organization.

The word "healthy" comes from the same root as the words "whole" and "holy". The holy fool Nasrudin shows that the way to be healthy is to embrace the whole of life.

Stress

Nasrudin looked very tired and anxious. His concerned colleagues asked him:

"Is there something worrying you?"

"Listen," retorted Nasrudin, "I have so many worries that if something awful happened today, I would not have time to worry about it for another six weeks."

I hope I am very ill

One day Nasrudin went running into the waiting room of the company doctor's surgery shouting:

"I HOPE I AM VERY ILL! I HOPE I AM VERY ILL!"

Everybody thought that he had finally taken complete leave of his senses and so they let him go in first to see the doctor.

As he went into the surgery he was still saying:

"I hope I am very ill! I hope I am very ill!"

"Why does anybody want to be very ill?" enquired the doctor.

Nasrudin responded, "Well, I would hate to think that anybody who felt as awful as I do, was actually well."

Burn-out

When he was old but still working very long hours, Nasrudin was asked how he had personally avoided the problem of "burn-out".

"It is quite simple," he replied. "I have spent all my life looking for the spark that would set me alight. While attending to the fire starting, you never have the problem of the fire burning out."

Reincarnation

Nasrudin was asked what he would like to be reincarnated as – a Buddha, a Llama, or a tiger or other animal. He replied:

"A snail, because a snail has the one thing I most lack."

"What is that?" they enquired.

"Time."

15

Die before you die

SOGYAL Rimpoche, the Tibetan teacher, once shocked an English audience by beginning his address on the subject of death by saying in his high-pitched voice:

> "Funny thing death, we think that it comes at the end of our life, but it doesn't, it comes in the middle. Well, we think it is the middle, but it is not, it is the end."

Like Nasrudin, he was purposefully disturbing our western mind set. A mindset that tries to banish death from the midst of life and hide it, out of sight, at the end of life. Rimpoche went on to tell the story of his Tibetan spiritual teacher, who when on a visit to New York was approached by a woman saying, "Lama, Lama, what shall I do? I am dying." His teacher replied, "You too are dying." The woman was incensed. "You do not understand, I have only six months to live!" At this point in the story Rimpoche pointed out that it was interesting that so many people in the west were told they had six months to live, and he never met anyone who was told they had four and a half months or seven months and three days! His teacher replied to the lady, "Madam, you cannot guarantee that you will die before me."

The phrase "Die before you die" is one of the most powerful in the Koran and challenges us to return death back to where it belongs, in the middle of life. Socrates said that philosophy was about practicing dying. The more one can embrace death in the midst of life, the more one can experience the fullness of life. For life and death are two faces of the same reality.

Jesus also talked of the need to die to oneself, in order to have eternal life. Yet so much of western life is about clinging to material life, surrounding ourselves with material things that give us the illusion of permanency and control. One small aspect of this in the world of business is that one can find hundreds of books on team building and establishing new teams, but hardly a book on effective team ending. In my experience, so many teams are burdened by unfinished business from previous teams that have never attended to their ending.

Nasrudin confronts our denial of death. In his own unique way he gives us a glimpse of the duality defying paradox: that to die is to live and to live is to die.

Knowing when and where to die

One day Nasrudin was telling stories of how marvelous both his father and grandfather were. Those listening were unimpressed until he told them that his grandfather was so wise that he knew the exact time and the exact place that he would die.

"What amazing foresight!" "What extraordinary awareness!" they were all remarking.

Eventually one curious listener asked, "How did your

grandfather know about where and when he would die?"

Nasrudin replied, "It was quite easy, the judge that passed sentence, told him."

After history

Nasrudin was excited to discover a book with the title *The End of History*. Having read the book he wrote to the publisher offering to write the sequel, to be entitled:

The End of History Part 2: What Happened Next.

The will

When Nasrudin was getting old, his lawyer asked him whether he had written his will?

"Indeed I have," replied Nasrudin. "As the only thing I still want is good health, I have left everything I have to the doctor who saves my life."

The addictive process

A seminar of aspiring leaders were interested in how addiction processes affected organizations.

"Tell us about addiction, Nasrudin?" they said.

He replied:

"First, just let me tell you three more stories ..."

Telling tales: the positive use of stories in organisations

A computer enthusiast searched out the latest and most powerful computer in the world, and programmed it to answer the question, whether or not computers would be able to think like human beings. After a very long wait the computer printer started to hum and the enthusiast rushed over to watch what was the answer the computer was printing. There on the paper were the words:

"Now that reminds me of a story..."

Stories constitute one of the fundamental languages that all human beings use to communicate what cannot be said through straight description. Gregory Bateson, who relates the story at the beginning of this chapter (Bateson 1975), goes on to describe stories as the "royal road to understanding relationship". He explores how, in the western, post-scientific world, most of our language has become the language of things, which is the language of defining material objects. This is an important and useful language when used in the service of the empirical study of the material world, but a most inadequate language for conveying relationship or the underlying patterns that permeate human existence.

As far as human history stretches back we find stories being told. What is more, many of these stories from other times and places, very different to our own, can still speak to us even though our "worlds" may be very different. The stories of Lao Tsu, the American Indians, those collected by the Brothers Grimm, or told by Scheherazade, those of the early Zen masters,

Jesus Christ and many other great story tellers can illuminate how we see the world around us now. This is because they speak not of things, but of the pattern of relationships that connects things. These stories are about the activities of dance, and of relationships.

But not all stories are timeless and speak of the universal beliefs, like those that are mentioned above. Some stories are more localized. Often stories start as anecdotes, or jokes told between friends. Only some of these take root and become repeated to a wider network, flowering as sagas or gossip through out the village or the organization. In time these can become the tribe's local myths; the stories it passes on to the next generation, to educate the new arrivals, not in the rules and laws of the tribe but in the unwritten "ways of doing things around here".

These stories not only become the vehicles for the group's unwritten rules, but also the means of educating the members of the group in how to pattern and make sense of what they experience in the group, be it a tribe, an organization or a family. For the culture resides, not just in the behavior, but also in the collective way of perceiving the world.

If we want to understand another culture, we need to listen to the stories it tells itself, not what it presents to foreign tourists. When working as a consultant to unearth the culture of an organization, I need to find a way of entering the internal storytelling circles. Direct inquiry will usually fail, as the culturally powerful stories are imbibed and become part of the way of being and perceiving, and thus no longer consciously noticed. I will have to inquire paradoxically and from the side. For this purpose I use such questions as:

"Can you produce a ten minute 'unofficial induction programme' that includes everything I would need to know in order to get on in this organization, but which nobody will tell me officially?"

"What are the jokes that most people know in this place, but you would not tell in public? "

"Who are the people that get talked about in this organization? What are the stories of villains, heroes, heroines and fools,that are told? What would I have to do to become a hero, villain or a fool here?"

Having gained privileged access to the inner world of story within a family, tribe or organization, it is important that I treat the stories with respect and neither rape them for data, nor translate them into the world of literal description and scientific analysis. Like dreams, stories speak their own language and cannot be immediately translated. Stories should be explored in their own terms and responded to in their own language. Together with my colleague Peter Reason, I spent some time in experimenting with how to explore stories within the language and medium of stories. The story of this search is written up in our joint paper "Inquiry through Storytelling" (Reason and Hawkins 1988).

Stories need to be played with, their pattern needs to be experienced and their rhythms need to be felt by the body. Stories cannot be fully understood from outside, but only through letting yourself enter the story, or by letting the story enter into your body.

So stories are a way of transmitting the culture to those that follow you and a way that any group has of defining its collective being. Every group and organization needs to have a culture and without it, collective functioning would become as impossible as individual functioning would be for an individual who has no firm personality. The difficulty with an organization's culture (or for that matter with an individual's personality) is that they become more fixed than is useful. For the culture of an organization needs not only to provide constancy of identity, but also flexibility of evolving in relation to a changing internal and external environment. But it is very hard to change what you are part of and cannot see. Your attempts to change the culture are almost certainly going to come from within the culture you are trying to change. A real catch 22.

The Chinese have an old proverb that "the last one to know about the sea is the fish". If you want to change the culture you are immersed within, you first have to become flying fish! So what is it that makes the salmon leap? Or in this case, what jolts the person out of their normal way of perceiving their familiar world?

In the same way that stories are conveyors of cultures, other stories can shock us from our ingrained ways of patterning our existence. I have written, elsewhere, a paper on "The Changing View of Learning" (Hawkins 1992), in which I argue that to create learning organizations we have to fundamentally shift our personal and collective ways of learning and to shift our theories of knowledge, our ways of knowing about the world. In this paper I describe some of the classic blocks to our learning about the world we live in and about the nature of change. These blocks include:

- Always seeing "things", rather than connecting patterns
- Constantly inferring linear causality, which leads to hunting for the thing or person that is responsible. The

root cause is usually attacked and the person blamed

- Nominalising processes so they become events
- Reducing multiple possibilities to dualistic, "either-or" choices
- Not including oneself in the field that one is trying to explore and therefore always locating the problem outside of oneself
- Locating relationship processes as properties that reside inside of individuals, or teams or organizations. Thus learning is seen as something you possess within you. The same applies to character traits at the individual level, or team dynamics at the team level, or organizational culture at the organizational level.

Most of the models and programs produced by the "Gurus" of the world of organizational development, are translated by those who try and apply them, into the language of their traditional mindset and the language of the existing organizational culture. This ensures that they just produce more of the same, another round of the organization's ingrained process. Thus, many good new ideas and approaches, become tomorrow's discarded "flavors of the month"; another initiative which seemed very exciting when it was started but fizzled out with disappointment and cynicism.

In this book I have poked fun at many of the popular organizational development approaches, not because I think that they are fundamentally flawed, but because the slavish, undigested application of them will always fail to bring about any sustained change. We are always more likely to blame the food than our process of eating for the resulting indigestion or sickness. Sheldon Kopp wrote a beautifully entertaining book entitled *If you meet the Buddha on the Road, Kill Him* (Kopp 1974). Nasrudin, in his wisdom, might well utter a similar phrase, "If you meet the perfect organizational development Guru at a conference, eat him, and spit out the seduction."

Not that the problem with the Gurus lies entirely with how they are applied: they too can be trapped within the mindsets they are trying to address in others. It can be hard for Argyris and Schon (1974, 1978) to double-loop their own theory of "double-loop learning", or for Peter Senge (1990) not to lecture on how important it is to create dialogue, rather than monologue or discussion. All of us who write in this field are liable to have a split between our medium and our message, between our rhetoric and the reality we create around us.

Mindsets are as ingrained in management consultants as they are in the organizations they try and help, for these mindsets are also part of the whole culture of the positivistic scientific world in which we have grown up and been educated.

Nasrudin's theory of knowledge is of a very different type. The logic of his stories are wired to a different pattern to that of our usual mindsets. Thus, when we let the story enter into our being, it can blow a fuse in our mindsets or make a short circuit of mental energy that jumps across the usual mental pathways. However, it is all too easy to enjoy the story, assimilate the shock and return to normal. The temporary disturbance that accompanies the humor can be buried away, and "normal service" reinstated.

If we really want the stories of Nasrudin to do their work, we have to invite him in, rather than let him merely entertain us on the doorstep. Having accepted him as a permanent guest, we can then start to tell and re-tell his stories, and watch and learn as they continue to work on us, each re-telling often disclosing a fresh perspective.

I am often told by other people that they can never remember jokes or stories. To some I have merely sympathized politely with their misfortune, while others I have suggested that remembering stories does not come from listening to them, but from re-telling them. I suggest (as I did in the introduction to this book) that they take a story that has some resonance for them and re-tell this story to three different people or groups, in three different settings, within the next twenty-four hours. They usually find that afterwards, that particular story and that aspect of the Nasrudin theory, has taken up lodgings within them.

If we just stay at the level of the storyteller, we are in danger of becoming merely the merchant of cleverness and the entertainer of mind games. It is only when we allow Nasrudin to become a personal companion, the irritating fool by our side, that we begin to accept him as our teacher. Then when, as leaders within an organization or as consultants to organizations, we are caught in the weeds of complexity, and the problem we are trying to sort out is entangled with our ways of perceiving it, we can turn to the internal Nasrudin, and ask him to yank us out of the weeds. "How would you see this situation?" we can ask him. Alternatively we can create a Nasrudin story about the situation, ensuring that we follow the disciplines.

These disciplines include:

- Ensuring that we are part of what is laughed at. The joke must partly be on us.
- That the ending is unexpected. We must make it surprising. This usually means that the first ending we create is from our own mindset and not Nasrudin's.

- That the story has an aftertaste. The difference between mere entertainment or distraction, and mutative humor, is that the former may delight us at the time, but will leave us empty, while the latter will disturb us for some time afterwards. This disturbance has the power to refresh our way of perceiving the world, as well as our mental digestion system.

These attributes do not just reside within the story, for storytelling is a process, and not a thing. Storytelling requires at least three active ingredients – a storyteller, a listener, and a story that plays between them. Each of these three ingredients work upon each other, sometimes successfully creating humor and learning, while at other times the cake goes flat. When a story fails to work, it is usually good feedback that there is not an alignment between the three elements, the storyteller, the story and the listener. The wise storyteller can incorporate this feedback and shift sideways to a new story, one that they have selected in relation to the response they have heard. Alternatively they may recognize that they need to shut up.

Now that reminds me of a story...

Bibliography

Books of Nasrudin stories

Anon. *Nasreddin Hodja*, Published by Siparis Isteme Adresi and Mahmet Ali Birand. Ankara, Istanbul.

Shah, Idries *The Exploits of the Incomparable Mulla Nasrudin*, Octagon Press. London, 1966.

Shah, Idries. *The Pleasantries of the Incredible Mulla Masrudin*, Jonathan Cape, London, 1968.

Shah, Idries. *The Subtleties of the Inimitable Mulla Nasrudin*, Octagon Press, London, 1973.

Shah, Idries, *The World of Nasrudin*, Octagon Press, London, 2003.

Stories can also be found in the following

Feldman, C. and Kornfield J. *Stories of the Spirit and Stories of the Heart*, Harper, San Francisco, 1991.

Ornstein, R. *The Psychology of Conscious*, Jonathan Cape and also Penguin Books, London, 1975.

Shah, Idries *The Sufis*, Doubleday & Company, New York, 1964.

Simac, Raoul *In a Naqshbandi Circle* Chapter 3 in Shah, I. (ed.) *The World of the Sufi*, Octagon, London, 1979.

Other references

Argyris, C. and Schon, D. *Theory in Practice*, Josey Bass. San Francisco,. CA, 1974.

Argyris, C. and Schon, D. *Organizational Learning*, Addison-Wesley, Reading, MA, 1978.

Badaracco, J.L. *Leading Quietly: An Unorthodox Guide to Doing the Right Thing*, Harvard Business School Press, Boston, MA, 2002.

Bateson, G. *Steps to an Ecology of Mind*, Palladin, London, 1973.

Bateson, G. *What is Epistemology?* Tape of a talk given at the Esalen Institute, Big Sur, CA, U.S.A, 1975.

Bennis,W. and Biederman, P.W. *Organizing Genius: the Secrets of Creative Collaboration*, Addison-Wesley, Reading, MA, 1996.

Bohm, D. *On Dialogue*. Routledge, London,1996.

DeMarco, T. *Slack: Getting past burnout, busywork and the myth of total efficiency*, Doubleday, New York, 2002.

Gemmill, G. and Oakley, J. "Leadership: An alienating social myth?" *Human Relations*, Vol: 45, pp.113-129, 1992.

Hamel, G and Prahalad, C.K. *Competing for the Future*, Harvard University Press Cambridge, MA, 1994.

Hampden-Turner, C. *Charting the Corporate Mind: From Dilemma to Strategey*, Basil Blackwell, Oxford, UK, 1990.

Hawkins, P. *The Spiritual Dimension of the Learning Organisation*, Management Education and Development 22(3) 166-81, 1991.

Hawkins, P. "The Changing View of Learning." Paper given at the 1st Learning Company Conference, University of Warwick, 1992. Published in *Towards the Learning Company* edited by Burgoyne, J., Pedler, P. & Boydell, T. McGraw-Hill. London, 1994.

Hawkins, P and Shohet, R. *Supervision in the Helping Professions*, Open University Press, Buckingham, 2000.

Hedberg, B. "How Organizations Learn and Unlearn" in P.C. Nystrom and W.H. Starbuck (eds) *Handbook of Organisational Design* Vol 1, Oxford University Press,1981.

Khan, Hazrat Inayat. *The Sufi Message* (Vol. IV). Barrie & Jenkins, London, 1972.

Kopp, S. *If you Meet the Buddha on the Road, Kill Him*, Sheldon Press. 1974.

Krishnamurti, J. *The First and Last Freedom*, Victor Gollancz, London, 1954.

March, J.G. and Olsen, J.P. *Ambiguity and Choice in Organizations*, Universitetsforlaget. Bergen, 1976.

Peters, T.J. and Waterman, R.H. *In Search of Excellence* , Harper & Row, New York, 1982.

Reason, P. and Hawkins, P. "Inquiry Through Storytelling" in Reason, P (ed.) *Human Inquiry in Action,* Sage, London, 1988.

Sample, S. *The Contrarian's Guide to Leadership*, Josey-Bass, San Francisco, 2002.

Senge, P. *The Fifth Discipline: the Art and Practice of the Learning Organisation*, Doubleday, New York, 1990.

Torbert, W. *Action Inquiry: the Secrets of Timely and Transforming Leadership*, Berret Koehler, San Francisco, 2004.

Look out for Nasrudin

WE are planning to publish a second volume of Nasrudin stories and would very much welcome responses to this first book. Please do write and tell us which stories you particularly enjoyed; how you have used the stories and what your explorations have led to.

We would also like readers to keep their eyes, ears and hearts open, for the appearance of new Nasrudin stories. They may appear in many guises and come from many different traditions and settings, but must follow the disciplines and structure that are outlined in the final chapter.

Please do send in any stories you find, inside or outside you. The origin of all stories that are included in the next volume will be acknowledged. The originators of all stories used, will in addition receive a free copy of both books and there will be a cash prize for the best story sent in and maybe even a donkey that you can only ride backwards!!

All correspondence should be sent to:
Peter Hawkins, Bath Consultancy Group
24 Gay Street
Bath BA1 2PD
UK

Telephone: 44 + (O)1225-333737
Fax: 44 + (O)1225-333738
e-mail: Peter.Hawkins@bathconsultancygroup.com

New stories will also be found on the special Nasrudin website:

www.nasrudin.org.

Bath Consultancy Group is an international consultancy organization specializing in helping all types of organizations to manage change. In addition, it runs conferences and training workshops in advanced consultancy skills. Information on any aspects of its work can be obtained from the above address or from:

www.bathconsultancygroup.com.